Namaqualand

North-west of Cape Town lies a seemingly barren and indifferent stretch of land that belies the great interest it evokes. For, once a year – lasting perhaps only three or four weeks – literally hundreds of kilometres of the countryside aré transformed into a blaze of flowers in what constitutes one of the floral wonders of the world. This is the fascination of Namaqualand.

2. *Heliophila coronopifolia* (Wild Flax)

3. *Gorteria diffusa* (Beetle Daisy)

4. *Grielum humifusum* (Duikerwortel)

5. In the Cederberg *Aponogeton distachyos* (Waterblommetjie or Cape Hawthorn) provide a colourful cover for ponds

6. *Dimorphotheca cuneata*

The area is subject to harsh conditions. Scorching sun and dry desert winds dehydrate the land and the people, and the rainfall ranges from a meagre 20 millimetres to no more than 230 millimetres a year. Yet even this amount, provided it falls in autumn or early winter, is enough to ensure fields bursting with colour in spring. Then botanists, horticulturists, gardeners and nature lovers flock to the area to admire and marvel.

Daisies are virtually synonymous with Namaqualand. In fact one annual species, *Dimorphotheca sinuata*, is so common to the area it is known as the Namaqualand Daisy. These shimmering brilliant flowers are best approached with the sun behind as they open facing the sun – and then only between mid-morning and mid-afternoon. A shrubby, perennial species, *Dimorphotheca cuneata*, with porcelain white flowers, is common in parts of the western Karoo. Vast stretches of purple and mauve Wild Cineraria (*Senecio elegans*) blend with blue or white Flax (*Heliophila*) or soften the bright golden Wild Camomile (*Pentzia grandiflora*). The yellow Duikerwortel (*Grie-*

7. *Romulea sabulosa* (Satin Flower)

8. *Dorotheanthus bellidiformis* (Bokbaaivygie)

9. *Dorotheanthus bellidiformis* (Bokbaaivygie)

10. *Cyanella alba*

11. *Drosanthemum speciosum*

12. A magnificent drift of white *Heliophila* (Wild Flax) carpets the ground like snow

13. *Drosera cistiflora* (Sundew)

14. *Pentzia grandiflora* (Wild Camomile)

15. *Hesperantha vaginata* (Evening Flower)

lum humifusum) is also widespread and often grows in combination with *Gorteria diffusa*. This deep orange flower derives its common name, Beetle Daisy, from three tiny green petals at its centre which are said to resemble a beetle. Some believe this attracts beetles to the flower and thus helps pollination.

Geology, topography and rainfall divide Namaqualand into different regions, each with its subtle changes in plant life. The sandy terrain of the Sandveld, for example, is for the most part only able to support succulents. Dew and moisture, from the early-morning mists rolling off the Atlantic Ocean, supplement this coastal region's extremely poor rainfall and enable the Sandveld to host the very colourful *Dorotheanthus bellidiformis* – most commonly known by the Afrikaans name Bokbaaivygie, though the English name, Livingstone Daisy, is also used.

Conditions change quite drastically a short distance from Namaqualand. In the nearby Cederberg one can see ponds covered in beautiful *waterblommetjies* (*Aponogeton*), the flowerheads of which are used with mutton to make a delicious stew called *waterblommetjiebredie*.

16. *Heliophila* (Blue Flax)

18. *Ursinia anthemoides* (Yellow Marigold)

17. *Senecio elegans* (Wild Cineraria)

19. *Ornithogalum dubium* (Chincherinchee)

Succulents

North of Springbok and into the Richtersveld below the last bend of the Orange River, the terrain grows increasingly stark and forlorn. Colourful flowers grow ever fewer, to be replaced by the Kokerboom (*Aloe dichotoma*) and aloes. In this north-western region of the Cape, as well as in the Little Karoo and the dry valleys of the eastern Cape and the Transvaal lowlands, only the hardiest of plants, adapted to the baking sun and dry, ungiving soil, can survive. They have done so in the most astonishing and complex of ways. *Stapeliae*, for example, bloom for only a few days, during which time they give off a

20. *Stapelia gettleffi* (Carrion Flower)

21. *Aloe variegata* (Variegated Aloe)

22. *Cheirodopsis peculiaris*

23. *Conicosia pugioniformis* (Pigsroot)

24. *Aloe dichotoma* (Kokerboom)

25. *Lithops bella* (Stone Plant)

26. *Pleispilos bolusii*

27. *Dactylopsis digitata* (Finger Plant)

29. *Huernia zebrina*

28. *Trichocaulon kubusense* (Gaap)

smell like rotting meat. This attracts flies which then pollinate the flower – hence the plant's common name of Carrion Flower. The extremely drought-resistant Pigsroot (*Conicosia pugioniformis*) similarly attracts flies and midges to its silky yellow flowers, while the showy *Cheiridopsis peculiaris* tries to evade the searing summer sun with its protective membrane.

Perhaps the strangest of the succulents are the stone plants, or *Lithops*. They lie half-buried in the ground, virtually indistinguishable from the stones and pebbles that surround them. A stone plant consists of an oval- or cylindrical-looking body formed by two leaves joined together. From a cleft across the centre a single yellow or white flower blossoms in spring. Some lithops have transparent tops which let in light.

As in other parts of South Africa where the climate is hostile, these plants continually adapt to their conditions. Many do not germinate every year, which avoids the possibility of all being eradicated during one exceptionally dry season.

Cape fynbos

The Cape region forms one of the six floral kingdoms of the world, and the area is amazing for the richness and profusion of its flora. The Cape *fynbos* as it is known (literally 'fine bush' or scrub), is composed primarily of proteas, heath-like ericas and reeds.

Some 350 species of the world-famous protea family grow in South Africa and more than half of them are found in the Cape. Most of them are protected plants. The Giant Protea (*Protea cynaroides*) has earned its place as the king of flowers and the country's national emblem, for its deep pink colour and magnificent 30-centimetre flowerhead make it an impressive specimen indeed. The proteas are also noted for the great variety of their shapes, from the delicate Pincushion Protea (*Leucospermum cordifolium*) to the rarer Blushing Bride (*Serruria florida*). In fact, they are named after the Greek god Proteus, who had the ability to take on an infinite number of shapes.

Ericas form the most important component of fynbos. While they do occur in other countries, a significant number – some

30. *Disa uniflora* (Pride of Table Mountain)

31. *Protea cynaroides* (Giant Protea)

32. *Erica baccans* (Berry Heath) on the hillside overlooking the Sentinel and Hout Bay

33. *Protea neriifolia* (Black Bearded Protea)

34. A protea beetle buries itself in a *Leucospermum conocarpodendron*

35. *Leucospermum cordifolium* (Pincushion Protea)

36. *Erica decora* (Sticky Rose Heath)

37. *Disa uniflora* (Pride of Table Mountain)

610 of the 640 species found in South Africa – are indigenous only to this country. Ericas are adapted to a wide range of conditions, growing on mountains, along streams, in swamps and on open terrain, and one or other species seems always to be in flower.

The average flower enthusiast is unlikely to see the elusive Pride of Table Mountain, unless willing to do some hiking, for *Disa uniflora* is found only near mountain streams and waterfalls. However, this fragile, protected member of the orchid family has been successfully cultivated at Kirstenbosch Botanic Gardens in the Cape.

Plants from the iris family are also included in fynbos and are well-represented by various species of gladiolus and watsonia. Watsonia are unusual in that many species – *W. comptonii* in particular – flower profusely after a fire.

Most of the flowers that comprise Cape fynbos are protected, as many of them (as well as a significant number of other flowers in South Africa) are in danger of becoming extinct.

38. *Watsonia comptonii* (Compton's Watsonia)

39. *Pterygedium catholicum* (Oumakappie)

40. *Herschelia graminifolia* (Blue Disa)

41. *Gladiolus debilis* (Painted Lady)

42. *Adenandra umbellata* (Shepherd's Delight)

43. *Crassula coccinea* (Red Crassula)

44. A bed of *Watsonia pyramidata* (Pink Watsonia) at Kirstenbosch Botanic Gardens

45. Pink *Watsonia pyramidata* and blue *Aristea major*

46. *Gladiolus carneus* (Bergpypie)

47. *Kniphofia uvaria* (Red-Hot Poker)

48. *Nerine sarniensis* (Guernsey Lily)

49. *Erica cerinthoides* (Red Erica)

50. *Agapanthus africanus* (Agapanthus)

51. *Leucospermum cordifolium* (Pincushion Protea)

52. *Gladiolus carmineus*

The Garden Route

Fynbos is not restricted to the Cape Peninsula. The term applies to vegetation that occurs both in the Peninsula and in a belt extending eastwards for several hundred kilometres along the coast, in an area known as the Garden Route. Rain falls fairly steadily throughout the year in this region, so flora is abundant and forests are lush. Proteas, ericas, watsonias and gladioli also grow here in great profusion, particularly in the George-Knysna area and on the mountain passes near George. With luck, the keen observer will see the rare and endangered George Lily (*Cyrtanthus purpureus*) on the mountains and in the forests. Further north, the magnificent Crane Flower (*Strelitzia reginae*) is found, and the succulent aloes begin to make an appearance.

An alternative route inland through the Little Karoo will reveal a landscape softened in winter and spring with the pink and crimson blossoms of the Chinese Lantern tree (*Nymania capensis*), a dominant feature of this area.

53. *Aloe arborescens* (Kransaalwyn)

54. *Erica cubica*

55. *Erica versicolor*

56. *Strelitzia reginae* (Crane Flower)

57. The rare *Cyrtanthus purpureus* (George Lily)

58. *Leucospermum cuneiforme* (Golden Pincushion)

59. *Aloe ferox* (Bitteraalwyn)

60. *Nymania capensis* (Chinese Lantern Tree)

61. *Watsonia longifolia*

62. *Serruria barbigera*

63. *Bidens formosa* (Cosmos) near Giant's Castle, Drakensberg

64. *Protea roupelliae* (Drakensberg Protea)

65. *Helichrysum sessile* (Everlasting)

66. *Brunsvigia natalensis* (Tumbleweed)

67. *Leonotis leonurus* (Wild Dagga)

68. *Kniphofia praecox* (Red-Hot Poker)

Drakensberg

Many of the flowers that are found in the Drakensberg grow in other parts of South Africa, but the spectacular scenery and great profusion of flora here make this region a worthwhile stop for anyone who wants to see some of the finest displays this country has to offer.

The Drakensberg's habitats range from warm valleys to peaks blanketed with snow for many months of the year, and from hot, dry slopes with little rainfall, to cool, moist ravines with mountain streams and waterfalls. Such changes in topography and climate enable this rugged mountain range to support a great diversity of plant life, from the hardy everlastings and ericas that survive the extremes of temperature on the summits, to the drifts of cosmos that gently climb the low-lying slopes and colour the roadsides.

Certain flowers, although not indigenous to this region only, are identified with the Drakensberg. They include the summer-flowering Drakensberg Protea (*Protea roupelliae*), the scarlet Natal or Drakensberg Bottlebrush (*Greyia sutherlandii*) and the well-known Wild Dagga (*Leonotis leonurus*), so called because the Zulus smoke its dried leaves. The plant is not related to *Cannabis*, however, and has no narcotic properties, although the tribesmen use it medicinally to treat colds and snake bites. Other popular flowers include Red-Hot Pokers (*Kniphofia*), also found on the summits, and the lovely watsonia, gladiolus and *Brunsvigia* species.

70. *Greyia sutherlandii* (Drakensberg Bottlebrush)

69. *Greyia sutherlandii* (Drakensberg Bottlebrush)

71. *Encephalartos ghellinckii* (Drakensberg cycad)

Natal

Many of the plants that occur in the Drakensberg are also encountered in the Natal area. Indeed, Natal shares much of the flora common to South Africa as a whole. Arum Lilies (*Zantedeschia aethiopica*) for example, which are found in abundance in ditches and along streams in the western Cape, also grow in the mountainous regions of Natal. The Dwarf Glory Bush (*Dissotis canescens*) is common to the eastern Transvaal and the Natal coast, and the fragrant Traveller's Joy (*Clematis brachiata*) is found throughout South Africa except in winter-rainfall areas.

72. *Clematis brachiata* (Traveller's Joy)

73. *Clivia miniata* (Bush Lily)

74. *Plectranthus ecklonii* (Spurflower)

75. *Gladiolus dalenii*

76. *Watsonia densiflora* (Natal Watsonia)

77. *Dissotis canescens* (Dwarf Glory Bush)

78. *Sandersonia aurantiaca* (Christmas Bells)

The most spectacular of Natal's flowers is the striking orange Bush Lily (*Clivia miniata*). It is one of only four species of *Clivia* endemic to South Africa, and is found in shady spots in forests. The appeal it holds for collectors has put it in danger of extinction and it is now protected, as is the Christmas Bell (*Sandersonia aurantiaca*), which is found in the Natal midlands and lowlands. Also protected is the Blood Lily (*Scadoxus multiflorus*), another forest dweller.

In general, although much of Natal's flora is common to other parts of the country, it is adapted to the warm, humid conditions of this sub-tropical region.

79. *Zantedeschia aethiopica* (White Arum Lily)

80. *Scadoxus multiflorus* (Blood Lily)

81. *Erythrina humeana* (Dwarf Coral Tree)

82. *Dais cotinifolia* (Pompon Tree)

83. *Rothmannia globosa* (September Bells)

84. *Crinum bulbispermum* (Orange River Lily)

Transvaal

The Transvaal is a dry area and the vegetation that grows here thrives on the region's hot days, crisp nights and summer rainfall. Aloes are seen in abundance, as are acacia trees, which most typify this part of the country – there are more than 40 indigenous species in South Africa. The Sickle Bush (*Dichrostachys cinerea*), which looks like an acacia but is distinguished by its unusual bi-coloured pink and yellow spiky flowers, is also fairly common. If used in outdoor cooking, the wood from this tree permeates food with toxic fumes capable of inducing severe headaches and nausea.

Flowering trees attract as much interest as flowers here; the famous Baobab tree (*Adansonia digitata*), found in the northeastern Transvaal and Kruger National Park, is a good example. The Baobab has exquisite white, scented flowers which are thought to be pollinated by bats. The pods contain seeds embedded in a spongy pulp that smells of sherbert. The fleshy stems contain a fair amount of liquid and, in dry periods, form an important source of moisture for animals. Another inhabitant of the Kruger National Park is the Impala Lily (*Adenium multiflorum*). Normally an insignificant drab shrub, in winter it produces spectacular white flowers which are fringed with red.

Other notable trees of this region include the Wild Pear

85. *Dichrostachys cinerea* (Sickle Bush)

86. *Burchellia bubalina* (Wild Pomegranate)

87. *Sterculia murex* (Lowveld Chestnut)

88. *Gerbera jamesonii* (Barberton Daisy)

89. *Aloe petricola* (Rock Aloe)

90. *Acacia karroo* (Sweet Thorn)

91. *Scadoxus puniceus* (Royal Paintbrush)

92. *Adansonia digitata* (Baobab)

93. *Adenium multiflorum* (Impala Lily)

94. *Dombeya rotundifolia* (Wild Pear)

95. *Bauhinia galpinii* (Pride-of-de-Kaap)

(*Dombeya rotundifolia*), which produces a magnificent display of white blossoms in late winter and spring, the Lowveld Chestnut (*Sterculia murex*), which doesn't have very significant flowers but is known rather for its decorative pods, and the Wild Pomegranate (*Burchellia bubalina*), which produces copious but scentless nectar that attracts numerous birds.

Among the well-known flowers of the Transvaal are the Flame Lily (*Gloriosa superba*), whose petals twist back to reveal brilliant shades of orange and yellow which resemble leaping flames, and the brilliant red Barberton Daisy (*Gerbera jamesonii*), a protected flower, indigenous only to the Barberton district and north-eastern Transvaal, but now commonly grown in gardens throughout South Africa.